D0394908

Rosa Parks

CIVIL RIGHTS PIONEER

By the Editors of TIME For Kids
WITH KAREN KELLAHER

Collins
An Imprint of HarperCollinsPublishers

About the Author: Karen Kellaher is the author of several biographies for young people and more than a dozen books for educators. She lives in rural New Jersey with her husband and three children.

Collins is an imprint of HarperCollins Publishers.

Library of Congress Cataloging-in-Publication Data is available.
ISBN-10: 0-06-057625-1 (trade) — ISBN-13: 978-0-06-057625-7 (trade)
ISBN-10: 0-06-057624-3 (pbk.) — ISBN-13: 978-0-06-057624-0 (pbk.)

1 2 3 4 5 6 7 8 9 10
First Edition

Photography and Illustration Credits:
Cover: AP Photo/Gene Herrick; cover inset: Time Life Pictures—Getty Images; cover flap: © 1976 Matt Herron—Take Stock; title page: National Archive; table of contents: AP Photo—Michael J. Samojeden; p.iv: Bettmann—Corbis; p.1: courtesy of Coach Crafters Inc.; p.2: AP Photo—Horace Cort; p.3: AP Photo; p.4: Corbis; p.5: Bettmann—Corbis; p.6: Bettmann—Corbis; p.7: Getty Images; p.8: Library of Congress; p.9: Corbis; p.10: AP Photo—Russell Lee; p.11: Granger Collection; p.12: Corbis; p.13: Corbis; p.14: Library of Congress; p.15: AP Photo; p.16: Corbis; p.17: Corbis; p.18: Time Life Pictures—Getty Images; p.19: Library of Congress; p.20: Highlander Research and Education Center; p.21: Library of Congress; p.22 (top): Library of Congress; p.22 (middle): Granger Collection; p.22 (bottom): Bettmann—Corbis; p.23: royalty free—Corbis; p.24: AP Photo; p.25: Raymond Gehman—Corbis; p.26: AP Photo—Gene Herrick; p.27: Time Life Pictures—Getty Images; p.28: Bettmann—Corbis; p.29: John Cravens—Time Life Pictures/Getty; p.30: Bettmann—Corbis; p.31: Bettmann—Corbis; p.32: AP Photo—Joe Holloway Jr.; p.33: Hulton Deutsch Collection—Corbis; p.34: AP Photo—Danny Johnston; p.35: Bruce Davidson—Magnum Photos; pp.36—37: *Detroit News*; p.38: Eli Reed—Magnum Photos; p.39: AP Photo—Joe Marquette; p.40: Martin H. Simon—Corbis; p.41: Kamenko Pajic—UPI/Landov; p.42: Newscom; p.43 (top): Punchstock; p.43 (bottom): AP Photo—Lawrence Jackson; p. 44 (top): Time Life Pictures—Getty Images; p. 44 (plane): Granger Collection; p.44 (kids): Bettmann—Corbis; p.44 (glasses): Corbis; back cover: William Philpott—Reuters

Acknowledgments:
For TIME For Kids: Editor in Chief: Jonathan Rosenbloom; Art Director: Rachel Smith; Designers: Michele Weisman and Colleen Pidel; Photography Editor: Sandy Perez Sanchez

 Find out more at www.timeforkids.com/bio/parks

Contents

▲ IN 1956 (the year this photo of Rosa was taken), black Americans were usually called "colored" or "Negro." The phrase "African American" became common in the 1980s.

CHAPTER 1

Tired of GIVING IN

On December 1, 1955, Rosa Parks stepped onto a bus—and into history.

For Rosa, that Thursday began like any other day. She went to work at a department store in Montgomery, Alabama. Rosa was a seamstress there. She fitted clothes for customers. Sometimes white customers were rude to her. Because Rosa was black, they did not see her as an equal. But Rosa couldn't defend herself, or she might get in trouble. So she stayed calm, kept quiet, and did her job.

> *"People always say that I didn't give up my seat because I was tired, but that isn't true. . . . No, the only tired I was, was tired of giving in."*
>
> —ROSA PARKS

▲ IN THE 1950s, only whites sat in the front seats of buses and trolleys in the South.

After work, Rosa boarded a city bus to go home. As always, she walked past the first five rows. These rows were empty, but they were marked "Whites Only." It was against the law for blacks to sit there. At that time Alabama and other southern states had laws that were unfair to black citizens. These segregation laws said that blacks had to drink from separate water fountains, go to separate schools, and ride in a separate part of the bus.

Rosa found a seat in the first row of the "Colored" section. Black passengers were allowed to sit there—unless white riders needed the seats.

As the bus continued, all the seats filled up. The driver noticed that a white man was standing. The driver looked at Rosa and the other black passengers.

"I want those seats," the driver said.

At first, no one moved. Then the man sitting beside Rosa moved to the back. The city's laws said that a black person could not sit in the same row as a white person. Rosa would have to move so that the white man could sit. But Rosa did not budge.

She was tired of giving in to unfair laws. And she was tired of being mistreated. Rosa had to stick up for herself.

"Are you going to stand up?" asked the driver.

"No," Rosa answered quietly.

"Well, I'm going to have you arrested," he warned.

Rosa looked the driver in the eye. "You may do that."

Soon two white police officers arrived. One of them asked Rosa why she hadn't given up her seat.

She asked him a question in return. "Why do you all push us around?"

"The law's the law, and you're under arrest," he answered.

Rosa hated segregation, and she hoped that the laws would change one day. But she did not know that her own act of courage would lead the way.

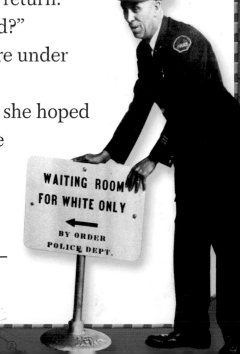

▶ THIS SIGN points the way for white bus passengers. Blacks waited in a separate area.

CHAPTER 2

Life on the FARM

Rosa was born on February 4, 1913, in Tuskegee, Alabama. Her parents were Leona and James McCauley. Leona was a teacher before Rosa was born. James was a carpenter.

Life was not easy for Rosa and her family. Her father often worked far away from home. He was gone for months at a time. Her mother stayed at home with baby Rosa. She missed her husband. She wished that he

▼ SOME BLACKS in the South owned farms like this. Rosa's grandparents had a small farm in Alabama.

would get a job close to home. But Rosa's father liked building houses and refused to quit. He and his wife often argued about his decision.

▲ IN THE SOUTH, entire families often worked the cotton fields. Young Rosa also picked cotton.

When Rosa was two, she and her parents moved in with her grandfather Sylvester and grandma Rose. They lived on a farm in the small town of Pine Level, Alabama. It was where Rosa's mother had grown up. Rosa's family was proud of the little farm. They were not rich, but they were the only black family in Pine Level to own land.

Rosa soon had a baby brother named Sylvester. But Rosa's parents still argued. Her father left the family and moved to another city. When Rosa was five years old, he came for a short visit. After that, Rosa did not see her father again until she was a grown-up.

A Close Family

To help support her family, Rosa's mother worked at a school that was eight miles from home. It was the closest teaching job she could find. The family did not own a car, so Rosa's mother stayed near school during

Scary NIGHTS

Rosa's grandfather often sat on the porch with a shotgun. He wanted to defend his family from the Ku Klux Klan, or KKK. Sometimes Rosa sat with him. She worried about her family.

The KKK is a secret organization of whites who hate blacks, Jews, and immigrants. It was formed after the Civil War. Klan members wore white robes and hoods to hide their faces. At night they set fire to black people's homes, barns, and churches. Sometimes they killed blacks.

Though the KKK is an illegal organization, it still exists today. Yet it is not as large or active as it was when Rosa was a girl.

the week. On weekends she came back to Pine Level and cared for her children. She took her kids to church and taught them at home. Rosa learned to read when she was only four years old.

Rosa missed her mother, but she loved living with her grandparents. She went fishing with them and helped on the farm. She collected eggs from the chickens and picked fruit and pecans from the trees. Sometimes Rosa pitched in on a neighbor's farm, too. She earned one dollar for every hundred pounds of cotton she picked.

When she was not working on the farm, Rosa enjoyed listening to her grandparents' stories. Both

of them had a lot to teach Rosa.

Grandfather Sylvester had been born a slave. When he was a boy, he was beaten by his owners. Sylvester never forgot the way he had been treated. He taught Rosa never to accept bad treatment from anyone.

Teaching Honesty

Grandma Rose also had been a slave. But she was treated well and grew up happy. She told Rosa not to judge people. She taught Rosa to be honest and respectful. So young Rosa usually did as she was told.

Rosa started school when she was six. The law said that blacks and whites had to go to separate schools. The school for white students was big and new. It had a lot of teachers. Rosa and the other black children in Pine Level went to a tiny one-room schoolhouse. There was one teacher for fifty students. Rosa liked learning and earned good grades. But she did not understand why everything was so unfair for blacks.

CHAPTER 3

Separate and UNEQUAL

When Rosa was eleven, her school in Pine Level closed. But Rosa's mother cared about her daughter's education. So she took a second job as a maid and saved her money. Then she sent Rosa to a private school for black girls.

The school was named the Montgomery Industrial School, but all the students called it Miss White's school. Miss Alice White was one of the founders and the principal.

▼ROSA left Pine Level for Alabama's state capital, Montgomery.

► MOST SCHOOLS for blacks (like this one) were overcrowded and lacked supplies. Miss White's school was better.

She was a white woman from the North who wanted to teach in the South. She believed that all Americans should have a good education.

Miss White's school was in Montgomery, the capital of Alabama. The city is twenty-five miles from Pine Level. Rosa had an aunt and cousins in Montgomery. She stayed with them while she went to school.

Rosa studied English, science, and other subjects. She took classes in cooking and sewing, too. Sewing was one of Rosa's favorite activities. She liked making her own dresses and aprons.

Outside of school, Rosa learned hard lessons about segregation. She knew a little about segregation already. In Pine Level, blacks and whites went to different schools and churches. But the town was too small to have segregated buses or trains. In Montgomery, almost everything was segregated. Blacks and whites had separate libraries, bathrooms, lunch counters, and phone booths.

▲ **BLACK PEOPLE** had to drink from separate water fountains, go through separate entrances in movie theaters and other public places, and eat in separate restaurants.

Why did Alabama and other states get away with treating blacks so unfairly? One reason was that the United States government said it was okay. In 1896 the U.S. Supreme Court ruled in favor of segregation in a case called *Plessy v. Ferguson*. Homer Plessy was a black man who had been arrested for sitting in the "white" part of a train. The court said that a state could make blacks and whites sit in separate train cars if the services in the cars were equal. This was known as the "separate but equal" rule. In reality, though, the services were hardly ever equal. Alabama and other states used the rule to get away with segregation in public places.

Changes Ahead

When Rosa was in ninth grade, Miss White's school closed. Rosa stayed in Montgomery and went to a black public junior high school. Then she went to the only black high school around. It was run by the Alabama State Teachers' College. Rosa dreamed of becoming a nurse or teacher.

But when Rosa was in eleventh grade, her Grandma Rose got sick. Rosa went home to care for her. But Grandma Rose soon died. Then Rosa's mother became ill, too. Rosa stayed home and nursed her mother back to health. Sadly, Rosa had to quit school. "It was just something that had to be done," she said later.

Fast Facts
THE ROARING '20S

For many Americans, the 1920s had brought big changes to the country:

☞ **Fashion:** Girls started to wear short skirts and bright lipstick. They also bobbed their long hair.

☞ **Dance:** Fast dances, such as the Charleston, became wildly popular. People even took part in dance marathons that didn't stop for days!

☞ **Transportation:** Many middle-class families owned automobiles for the first time.

☞ **Music:** People listened to jazz on their radios.

☞ **Entertainment:** The first movies with sound were made in 1927. They were called "talkies." Everyone loved to go to the movies now!

CHAPTER 4

Rosa GROWS UP

When Rosa was eighteen, she met someone who would change her life. Raymond Parks, who was called Parks for short, was ten years older than Rosa. He worked as a barber. At that time, barbershops were important gathering spots for black men. They would discuss politics and civil rights—the treatment of all people equally under the law. Parks had many friends and always knew what was happening in the city.

Parks fell in love with Rosa right away. He asked her to marry

▲ BARBERSHOPS WERE GATHERING PLACES for blacks to share local news and opinions.

▲ **RAYMOND PARKS** was active in the NAACP, a group fighting for civil rights.

him on their second date! But Rosa wanted to get to know him better. She soon discovered that Parks was one of the smartest people she had ever met. Parks was fun, too. He took Rosa for rides in his red sports car. Rosa finally married Parks two years later, in 1932.

Working Together

Parks helped Rosa achieve her dreams. He encouraged her to go back to high school. Rosa earned her diploma when she was twenty.

Parks also talked to Rosa about the National Association for the Advancement of Colored People. This was known as the NAACP. Parks was active in the organization. He was helping the NAACP fight for blacks' civil rights.

Rosa was curious about the NAACP. One night in 1943 she went to a meeting in Montgomery. The members welcomed Rosa and asked her to be the group's secretary. Rosa agreed. Now she had two jobs.

▲ **AN NAACP POSTER** from 1949 encourages people to join the group.

Can you PASS THE TEST?

Voting tests were one way that some states kept blacks from registering. If people wanted to vote, they had to pass a test—but only if they did not own land. Since many whites owned land, they didn't have to take the test.

The exam questions were difficult, and the test takers were not always told which ones they got wrong. Rosa was educated, and it still took her three tries before she passed the test!

To make voting even more difficult, blacks were often asked questions that were impossible to answer, such as: How many bubbles are in a bar of soap? How many seeds are in a watermelon? How many hairs are on a hog's back?

During the day, she worked as a secretary on an army base. At night she volunteered with the NAACP. She answered mail, organized meetings, and took notes. She also did work for E. D. Nixon, a local leader of the NAACP. The mistreatment of blacks had always bothered Rosa. Now she was doing something about it.

One issue that was especially important to Rosa was voting. She knew that voting meant power. If blacks could voice their opinions, politicians would have to listen to them. And then life for black people could improve. So Rosa joined the Montgomery Voters League. She and many other volunteers worked hard to help blacks register, or sign up, to vote.

▶ MANY BLACKS tried to register to vote but were told they couldn't.

How high is up? Questions like these were insulting and disrespectful.

Today all U.S. citizens over the age of eighteen are allowed to vote. They do not have to own land. And they do not have to take a test.

This was no easy job. Although blacks had the right to vote in Alabama, the rules often kept them from registering. For example, blacks were only allowed to sign up to vote on certain days and at certain hours—usually in the middle of the workday. But the biggest challenge was a test that blacks had to take before they could register.

These voting rules were unfair to all blacks. But they were especially unfair to black war veterans and soldiers. Rosa's brother, Sylvester, had just fought in World War II. He had risked his life for his country. But when he returned to the U.S., he was not even allowed to vote.

Rosa was angry. She firmly believed that everyone should be allowed to vote. And she was determined to help make that happen. Even though the KKK often killed people who helped blacks register, Rosa

▼ DURING WORLD WAR II, African Americans served in segregated units.

didn't let her fear stop her from volunteering.

Over time, Rosa found another way to help, too. She advised the NAACP Youth Council. The council was made up of black teens. She taught the teens to believe in themselves and to fight for their rights.

▲ MEMBERS of the NAACP Youth Council met to socialize and to fight for equal rights.

Battle on the Bus

One day in 1943, Rosa had an awful experience on a bus. She entered through the front door and paid her ten cents. The driver ordered Rosa to get off the bus and then get on again—this time using the back door. His order was perfectly legal. Drivers often enforced the law. Sometimes they even drove away while black passengers walked to the back door.

Rosa saw that it was very crowded near the back, so she stayed where she was. The driver walked over to her, grabbed her sleeve, and pushed her toward the door. Proud and angry, Rosa got off the bus and did not get back on. She didn't know the driver's name, but she'd remember his face. She would see him again twelve years later.

CHAPTER 5

Making HISTORY

As the years passed, Rosa stayed busy. She got a job as a seamstress at the Montgomery Fair department store. She also did some sewing work for a white couple, Virginia and Clifford Durr. Like Rosa, they believed that blacks should have the same rights as whites. Rosa and the couple became good friends.

Rosa also continued working with the NAACP and fighting for blacks' rights. In 1954 an important court

◄ **AN EXCELLENT** seamstress, Rosa earned her living repairing clothes.

► **LINDA BROWN**, whose father started an important court case, is the girl in the front row.

case caught her attention. It was called *Brown v. Board of Education.* In this famous case, a black couple in Topeka, Kansas, was angry that their daughter, Linda Brown, couldn't go to the white school near their house. After a long court battle, the U.S. Supreme Court ruled that states could no longer have separate schools for blacks and whites. Rosa was thrilled. If the court stopped segregation in schools, maybe it would stop segregation on buses, too. Rosa hoped these other changes would come soon.

One year after the big case, Rosa was invited to a ten-day workshop in Tennessee. The Highlander Folk School was run by people who wanted to make sure that school segregation really happened. Blacks and whites both attended the workshop. They ate together and talked together about ways to bring about change. This was the first place Rosa had ever been where

▲ **HIGHLANDER STUDENTS** enjoyed taking breaks together. Rosa is the woman behind the child.

blacks and whites were considered equals. She learned how to help people work for civil rights. She felt happy and hopeful.

Then Rosa went back to Montgomery and its unfair laws. This was very hard for her, but she went back to riding segregated buses. She didn't know that change would come so soon.

Rosa's Arrest

On December 1, 1955, Rosa left to go home after a hard day at work. She got on the Cleveland Avenue bus and deposited her fare. At first, she did not notice who was driving. Then she recognized the driver's face. He was the same man who had thrown her off the bus twelve years earlier. His name was James Blake.

The next few moments would change history. The bus filled, and the driver ordered Rosa to give up her seat to a white man. Rosa refused. She sat quietly while the driver called the police. When the officers arrived, they arrested Rosa and drove her to the police station. They took her photograph and fingerprints. Then they put her in a cell.

Two hours later, Rosa was allowed to call home. Clifford and Virginia Durr, E. D. Nixon, and her husband, Parks, all came to get her. The bail to get her out of jail was $100, which was a lot of money then. Rosa's friends paid the money and took her home.

Rosa would have to go to court on Monday, December 5. The court would decide if Rosa was guilty of breaking the segregation laws.

▼ AFTER ROSA'S ARREST, a police officer took her fingerprints.

Moving STORIES

Rosa Parks was not the first person to fight segregation on public transportation. Here's a look at some other pioneers who fought for fairness:

☞ **Sojourner Truth**

A conductor tried to push this former slave off a streetcar in Washington, D.C., in 1865. She got him fired.

☞ **Ida B. Wells**

In 1884 this black newspaper writer refused to leave a "whites only" train car in Tennessee. She was arrested.

☞ **Jackie Robinson**

In 1943 this army officer sat in the middle of a bus in Texas and refused to move. He was arrested and later found innocent. He became the first black to play in major league baseball.

A Big Plan

That night Rosa and her friends stayed up late talking. Nixon suggested that they should try to take Rosa's case to the U.S. Supreme Court. He and the NAACP would prove that the bus laws went against the Constitution—the highest law in the U.S. The Constitution says that everyone must be treated equally. If the Supreme Court decided that the bus laws went against the Constitution, the laws would have to change. This is what happened with *Brown v. Board of Education*, and it could happen again.

Nixon thought that Rosa was the perfect person to challenge the bus laws in court.

She was dignified and polite. And she wasn't afraid to speak up for herself.

But Rosa was not so sure about the plan. She did not like being in the spotlight. Her husband was worried, too. But finally Rosa agreed.

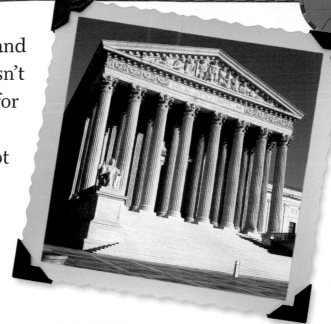

▲ **E. D. NIXON** thought Rosa's arrest was a good thing. If she was found guilty, her case could be challenged in the Supreme Court.

Nixon immediately began calling black leaders in the community to tell them about the plan. Soon the news reached a black professor named Jo Ann Robinson. She headed a group called the Women's Political Council. Robinson suggested that black leaders should start a boycott. They should encourage blacks to stay off the city buses on Monday, the day of Rosa's trial. The boycott would do three things. It would hurt the bus company. (About three-fourths of the city's bus riders were black. If they did not ride the buses, the company would lose money.) It would show support for Rosa. And it would show that blacks were tired of segregation—and determined to make changes.

CHAPTER 6

The Bus
BOYCOTT

*T*he night of Rosa's arrest, the Women's Political Council began organizing the one-day bus boycott. They printed 35,000 flyers to tell people about it. The flyers said, in part: *Don't ride the bus to work, to town, to school, or anywhere, on Monday, December 5. If you work, take a cab, share a ride, or walk.*

The next morning, council members distributed the flyers at schools and stores. Meanwhile, Nixon called the newspaper and the city's black leaders to help spread the word. By Friday evening, most people knew about the plan.

◄ DURING THE BUS BOYCOTT, some Montgomery citizens hitchhiked to work.

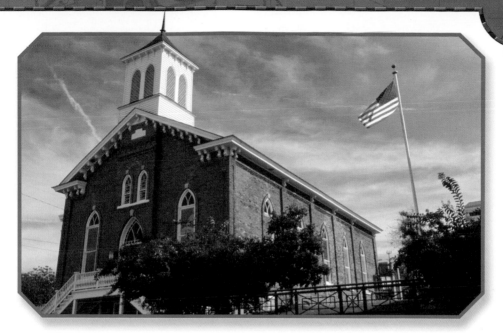

▲ MONTGOMERY'S Dexter Avenue Baptist Church became a meeting place for leaders of the boycott.

But Rosa's boycott had already begun. She had decided that she would never set foot on a segregated bus again. She took a cab instead of a bus to work that day. At lunchtime, she met with Fred Gray. He was the black lawyer hired by the NAACP to represent her. That weekend she met with leaders at the Dexter Avenue Baptist Church to go over the boycott plans. Everyone was ready.

On Monday, December 5, Rosa went to court. She was found guilty, and was ordered to pay a $14 fine. After the trial, Gray spoke to reporters. He said that the city's bus laws were unjust and that he would ask the U.S. Supreme Court to review Rosa's case. He also said that Rosa would not pay the fine.

▲ **MARTIN LUTHER KING JR.** encouraged the boycotters.

Outside, the boycott went on as planned. Blacks stayed off the buses. They walked or shared rides. Black cab owners helped out. They gave people rides for ten cents—the same price as a bus fare. Children ran behind some of the buses, shouting, "No riders today!" They were right. Montgomery's buses were nearly empty. The boycott was a success.

On Monday night, the black leaders met again to review how the boycott had gone. This time, nearly five thousand people arrived to show their support. They spilled out of the church and onto the sidewalk. Rosa attended the meeting and sat right up front with the boycott's leaders. When a minister introduced her, the crowd chanted her name and shouted their thanks.

Almost everyone agreed that the boycott had worked. They decided to continue it until the bus laws changed. The black leaders had chosen a young

Baptist minister to take charge of the boycott. His name was Dr. Martin Luther King Jr. Rosa admired the young preacher. The two of them became friends.

Dr. King gave a speech that night. "We are here this evening to say to those who have mistreated us so long that we are tired—tired of being segregated and humiliated," he said. The crowd stood and cheered.

The Boycott Gathers Support

The boycott was not easy. As weeks stretched into months, people had to find new ways to get to work and school. Some of them formed carpools. Some rode bikes. But most of them walked. They walked until their feet were sore. They walked until they wore out their shoes. People from all over the country heard

▼ RAINY WEATHER didn't keep people from walking to their jobs during the Montgomery bus boycott.

▲ ROSA speaks to a reporter after her second arrest. E. D. Nixon is standing beside her.

about the boycott. Many of them sent shoes and money to show their support.

The protest was especially hard for Rosa. She began to get phone calls from some angry whites. They blamed her for the "trouble" she was causing. Some even threatened to kill her. Rosa and her husband both lost their jobs. She was even arrested again. This time it was for boycotting! Montgomery city officials had dug up an old law that said boycotting was illegal. They also arrested hundreds of other boycotters. Still, Rosa's strength—and her belief that she was doing the right thing—kept her going.

Sweet Success

People could see that the boycott was working. The bus companies were losing money. So were some stores in town. Since blacks had stopped riding buses, they did not go downtown to shop. Business owners were getting worried.

Six months after the boycott began, good news arrived. The U.S. Supreme Court had agreed to review Rosa's case. Now the whole country waited to hear what the court would decide. Would it say that bus segregation was fair? Or would it vote to stop the unfair laws?

On November 13, 1956, the court made its decision. It ruled that segregation on city buses in Alabama was unconstitutional. Montgomery would have to stop separating blacks and whites on its buses. A few weeks later, on December 20, the U.S. Supreme Court delivered its order in writing. After 381 days, blacks once again boarded Montgomery's buses. But now they could sit wherever they chose.

▲ MARTIN LUTHER KING JR. and other boycott leaders wait to hear the Supreme Court's decision. The department store where Rosa worked is in the background.

CHAPTER 7

Out of the SPOTLIGHT

*I*n December of 1956, Rosa boarded a Montgomery city bus for the first time in more than a year. Rosa sat in the front row. She was happy that no one could ever ask her to move again. "When I declined to give up my seat, it was not that day, or bus,

in particular," Rosa said years later. "I just wanted to be free, like everybody else." Rosa was proud that she had

◄ **PHOTOGRAPHERS** asked Rosa Parks to pose on an integrated Montgomery bus.

▲ Students wave at an empty bus during a boycott in Tallahassee, Florida. These boycotts spread to cities all over the South.

helped to bring about important change—not just in Montgomery, but all over the South. Blacks in other cities saw what had happened in Montgomery. They began their own boycotts, marches, and protests. The civil rights movement was in full swing.

For a while, Rosa and her husband continued to live in Montgomery. Rosa kept working with the NAACP. She traveled to schools and churches all over the United States, speaking about her arrest and about civil rights. Still jobless, Rosa and Parks struggled to get by.

A Move North

By 1957 Rosa was ready for a change. She was still getting threats from people who were angry about her work, and she was tired of living in fear. Along with her husband and mother, she moved to Detroit, Michigan. Rosa's brother, Sylvester, had settled there years before.

In Detroit Rosa joined the local chapter of the NAACP. She continued to give speeches about her experiences. One day a college president heard Rosa speak. He offered her a job at the Hampton Institute in Virginia. Rosa would help manage the cleaning staff. She loved the idea of being around students, so she took the job. But since she could not find a job there for her husband, she moved back to Detroit after one year.

▲ ROSA moved to Detroit and continued to speak about civil rights.

▶ IN 1963 Martin Luther King Jr. led a civil rights march in Washington, D.C.

Rosa returned to volunteering with the NAACP. But she needed a job that paid money, too. So she found work as a seamstress in a clothing factory. There she made a new friend named Elaine Steele. Still in high school, Elaine was much younger than Rosa. But the two women would stay good friends for life.

Marching for Change

Rosa also kept in touch with a good friend, Dr. Martin Luther King Jr. He helped inspire Rosa to keep fighting for civil rights. In 1963, when Dr. King practiced his famous "I Have a Dream" speech in Detroit, Rosa was at his side. She then traveled to the nation's capital to see him deliver the speech. Dr. King spoke at the March on Washington on August 28 before hundreds of thousands of people.

Rosa and the other women there were not allowed to give speeches. They weren't even allowed to march

Mystery PERSON

☞ Clue 1: I was born in Hope, Arkansas, in 1946. The Montgomery Bus Boycott started when I was nine years old. My friends and I began riding in the back of the bus to honor Rosa Parks.

☞ Clue 2: As a high school student, I met President John F. Kennedy in Washington, D.C. I decided on a career in government. On my school debate team, I argued for better laws to protect blacks' civil rights.

☞ Clue 3: I became our nation's 42nd President and continued to support civil rights. In 1996 I presented the Presidential Medal of Freedom to Rosa Parks.

Who am I?

alongside the men, but they did have a separate procession. Civil rights leader Bayard Rustin introduced Rosa to the crowd. He said she was a woman who had made a difference in the civil rights struggle. To many Americans, Rosa symbolized dignity in the face of unfair treatment.

In 1965 Rosa took part in another march led by Dr. King. Thousands of people walked fifty miles in Alabama, from Selma to Montgomery. They marched to demand equal voting rights.

This was the second time they had tried to march to Montgomery. The first time there had

▶ **MARCHERS** from Selma to Montgomery called attention to the need for equal voting rights.

been so much violence that they had to turn back. The march took five days, and Rosa joined in for the final eight miles. When the march finally ended at the Montgomery capitol, there was a crowd of angry whites. A few months later, President Lyndon Johnson signed the Voting Rights Act, which made voting tests illegal. Yet there was still a long way to go until all people were treated with dignity and respect.

CHAPTER 8

Rosa's
GIFT TO US

*I*n 1965 Rosa got an exciting new job. She became an assistant to a black U.S. Congressman from Michigan named John Conyers. One of her responsibilities was to find housing for homeless people. Rosa felt good about her position and the fact that she was helping others.

But the next several years were hard for Rosa. She lost many people who were important to her. In 1968 Dr. King was assassinated. Her husband, Parks, died of cancer in 1977. Two years later her mother also

▶ ROSA was an honored guest at many events. She took part in this parade in 1976 in Detroit, Michigan.

passed away. At the age of sixty-six, Rosa moved into an apartment building for senior citizens. She was ready to begin the next chapter in her life.

Making a Difference

Rosa kept working to make the nation a better place. She was employed by Congressman Conyers until she was seventy-five years old. But Rosa wanted to do even more.

In 1987 Rosa created an organization called the Rosa and Raymond Parks Institute for Self Development. Elaine Steele helped her start the institute, which is still around today. It teaches teens

about African American history and assists them in finding jobs.

Together Rosa and Elaine took the students on field trips. On one trip they visited important places that were part of the Underground Railroad. (This was the secret network that southern slaves used to escape to freedom in the North in the mid-1800s.) On another trip Rosa took the teens to places that were important in the civil rights movement. Many people around the country gave money to help pay for these trips.

As Rosa got older, her health declined. She could no longer travel, march, or make speeches. She had to stop running the Parks Institute and asked Elaine to

◄ TEENS ENJOYED meeting Rosa and talking to her about her life.

take over for her. Rosa still struggled with money, but her friends chipped in to help her pay rent and other expenses.

Remembering a Heroine

The nation never forgot "the Mother of the Civil Rights Movement." All over the country, schools and streets were named for her. The Rosa Parks Library and Museum in Montgomery was built in her honor. Visitors can learn about her life there.

▲ **A PROUD ROSA** receives the Presidential Medal of Freedom from President Clinton.

Rosa also received many important awards and honors. In 1996 President William Clinton awarded Parks the Presidential Medal of Freedom for her contributions to civil rights. Three years later he presented her with the Congressional Gold Medal, the highest honor the U.S. government can give.

On October 24, 2005, Rosa died in her Detroit apartment at the age of ninety-two. Several close friends were at her side. News of her death saddened the nation, and many people planned special ways to say good-bye.

Hundreds of mourners attended a memorial in Montgomery, and thousands more celebrated Rosa's life at a service in Washington, D.C. For two days Rosa's coffin was placed inside the U.S. Capitol so that people could pay their respects. This is a tradition usually saved for Presidents and war heroes. Rosa was the first woman to receive this honor.

At the memorials, dozens of people spoke about Rosa's incredible life. The Reverend Jesse Jackson, an African American leader, gave a moving speech about Rosa. "She ignited a fire in this country," he said. "The world owes her a debt of gratitude."

▼ THOUSANDS of Americans paid their respects to Rosa Parks.

Rosa was laid to rest in a Detroit cemetery. She was buried next to her

▲ **A GRATEFUL WOMAN** holds a picture of Rosa at a memorial service.

husband, mother, and brother. On the day of her funeral, flags all over the nation were flown at half-staff. In Montgomery, Detroit, and other cities, the front seats of city buses were left empty to represent the nation's loss.

Over the years, Rosa Parks has served as a role model for many Americans. By staying seated on a bus, she stood up for what was fair and right. She showed that with courage and determination, one person can help change the world.

INTERVIEW

Talking About ROSA

▲ **John Conyers**

TIME FOR KIDS editor Kathryn Satterfield spoke with Congressman John Conyers about Rosa Parks, who worked in his Detroit, Michigan, office.

Q: How do you think the United States would be different if Rosa Parks had given up her seat on a bus?

A: That heroic act was an important moment in American history because the Supreme Court ruled that segregation on buses was against the law. The case led to other attacks on segregation and to the collapse of the segregated system that grew out of the Civil War itself.

Q: Do you think Rosa knew at the time that she was helping to start up the civil rights movement?

A: I don't think that she was planning something this big. It was just something that she knew she was going to do, and that was the day she did it. Her faith and her determination that this was the right thing to do guided her.

Q: What can kids learn from Rosa Parks's example?
A: Rosa Parks showed us that everybody counts. When we all decide to do something, it amounts to a wave of energy that can indeed change things. She taught us that nobody should be held back because of their skin color. Each individual is important and powerful. That was her gift to us.

▶ ROSA HELPED make it possible for people such as Secretary of State Condoleezza Rice and Senator Barack Obama to serve in government.

Rosa Parks's
KEY DATES

1913	Born on February 4, in Tuskegee, Alabama
1924	Moves to Montgomery
1932	Marries Raymond Parks
1943	Joins the NAACP
1955	Refuses to go to the back of the bus and is arrested, starting a bus boycott
1956	Sits in the front of a bus after bus segregation is ruled unconstitutional
1963	Attends the March on Washington
1999	Receives Congressional Gold Medal
2005	Dies on October 24, in Detroit, Michigan

1939 The jet airplane is invented.

1955 A new vaccine helps wipe out polio in the U.S.

2000 People around the world celebrate the start of the twenty-first century.